From Rubbish to Riches

Cardboard

Daniel Nunn

www.raintreepublishers.co.uk
Visit our website to find out
more information about
Raintree books.

To order:

☎ Phone 0845 6044371

🖹 Fax +44 (0) 1865 312263

🖳 Email myorders@raintreepublishers.co.uk

Customers from outside the UK please telephone +44 1865 312262

Raintree is an imprint of Capstone Global Library
Limited, a company incorporated in England and
Wales having its registered office at 7 Pilgrim Street,
London, EC4V 6LB – Registered company number:
6695582

Edited by Rebecca Rissman, Daniel Nunn, and
Sian Smith
Designed by Joanna Hinton-Malivoire
Picture research by Tracy Cummins
Originated by Capstone Global Library Ltd
Printed and bound in China by South China
Printing Company Ltd

ISBN 978 1 406 22678 2
15 14 13 12 11
10 9 8 7 6 5 4 3 2 1

British Library Cataloguing in Publication Data
Nunn, Daniel. Cardboard. – (From rubbish to riches)
1. Cardboard art 2. Paperboard-Recycling- 3. Trash
art 4. Refuse and refuse disposal 5. Salvage
745.5'9-dc22
A full catalogue record for this book is available
from the British Library.

Acknowledgements
We would like to thank the following for permission
to reproduce photographs: Getty Images pp. 9
(James Hardy), 17 (Flying Colours Ltd); Heinemann
Raintree pp. 6, 10, 11, 12, 13, 14, 15, 16, 18, 19, 20, 21,
23a, 23b, 23c, 23d, 23f (Karon Dubke); istockphoto
pp. 7 (© Rob Hill), 8 (© Petr Nad), 22a (© Muammer
Mujdat Uzel), 23e (© David Franklin); Shutterstock
pp. 4 (© Shawn Hempel), 5 (© Stephen Coburn),
22b (© James M. Phelps, Jr.), 22c (© ID1974).

Cover photograph of cardboard animals
reproduced with permission of Shutterstock
(© holbox). Cover inset image of a box reproduced
with permission of Shutterstock (johnnyscriv).
Back cover photographs of a cardboard spider
and a bird feeder reproduced with permission of
Heinemann Raintree (Karon Dubke).

Every effort has been made to contact copyright
holders of material reproduced in this book. Any
omissions will be rectified in subsequent printings if
notice is given to the publisher.

Contents

Some words are shown in bold, **like this**. You can find them in the glossary on page 23.

What is cardboard?

Cardboard is a **material** that is often used in **packaging**.

Cardboard is made of very thick paper.

When you buy something from a shop it often comes in a cardboard box.

Toys, eggs, and breakfast cereal can all come in cardboard boxes.

What happens when you throw cardboard away?

Cardboard is very useful.

But when you have finished with it, do you throw it away?

If so, then your cardboard will end up at a rubbish tip.

It will be buried in the ground and may stay there for a very long time.

What is recycling?

It is much better to **recycle** cardboard instead of throwing it away.

Separate cardboard from your other rubbish and then put it in a recycling bin.

The cardboard will be collected and taken to a **factory**.

Then the cardboard will be made into something new.

How can I reuse old cardboard?

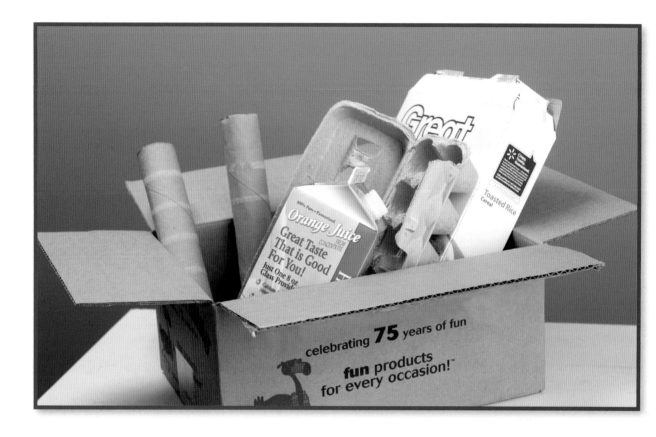

You can also use old cardboard to make your own new things.

When you have finished with a box or tube made of cardboard, put it somewhere safe.

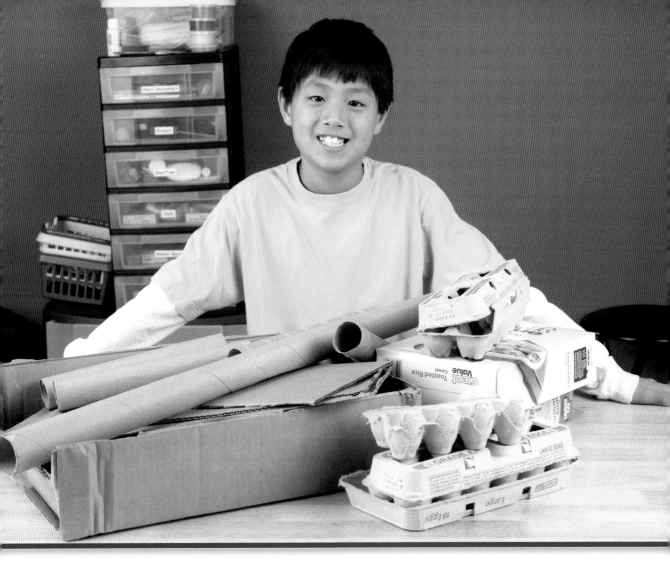

Soon you will have lots of cardboard waiting to be reused.

You are ready to turn your rubbish into riches!

What can I make with cardboard tubes?

Cardboard tubes are used to hold kitchen roll or wrapping paper.

But you can use them to make fun people puppets.

You can also use them to make your own musical instruments.

It is easy to make your own cardboard **kazoo**.

What can I make with egg boxes?

You can use an egg box to make your own indoor garden.

You can plant seeds in each cup.

Egg boxes can also be made into great model insects.

This spider, caterpillar, and ladybird have all been made from one egg box.

What can I make with cardboard boxes?

This milk **carton** has been made into a bird feeder.

You can use it to give food to birds in the winter.

Large cardboard boxes can be made into almost anything.

This box has been made into a house!

Make your own juice carton boat

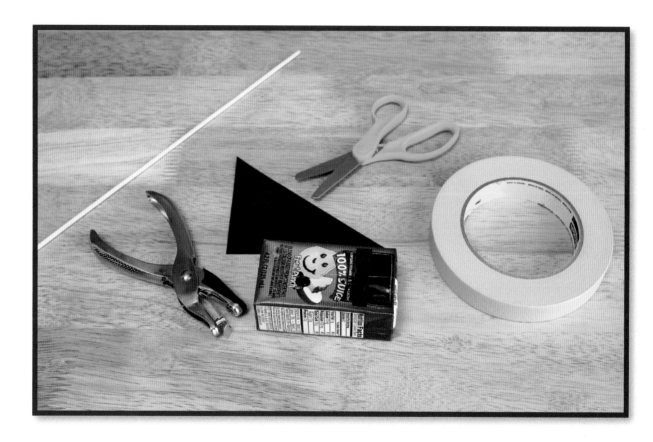

You can use an old juice **carton** to make your own boat.

You will need an empty juice carton, a stick, some card, sticky tape, scissors, and a hole punch.

First, cut a triangle out of the card and use the hole punch to make a hole at the top and bottom.

Next, slip the stick through the two holes in the triangle.

Use the sticky tape to cover the hole in the **carton** where the straw used to go.

Then use the stick to make a hole in the side of the carton.

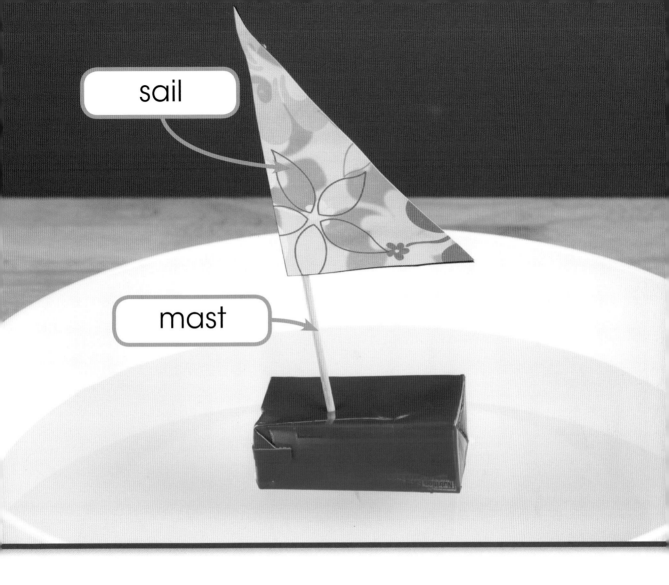

sail

mast

Push the stick through the hole in
the carton to make the sail and mast.

Decorate the boat and put it in water.
Blow on the sail to make your boat move!

Recycling quiz

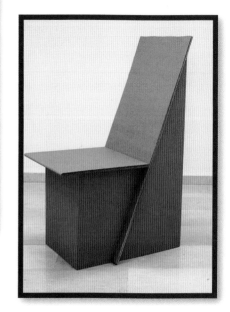

One of these photographs shows furniture made from **recycled** cardboard. Can you guess which one? (Answer on page 24.)

Glossary

 **carton** small cardboard box. Some cartons are covered with a special material that helps them to hold liquids.

 **factory** building where something is made

 **kazoo** musical instrument that makes a buzzing sound when you hum into it

 **material** what something is made of

 **packaging** box or wrapping that something comes in

 **recycle** break down a material and use it again to make something new

Find out more

Ask an adult to help you make fun things with cardboard using the websites below.

Animals: **www.enchantedlearning.com/crafts/ Eggcarton.shtml**

Bird feeder: **www.ziggityzoom.com/activities. php?a=302**

Kazoo: **www.makingfriends.com/music/kazoo.htm**

Puppets: **www.makingfriends.com/recycle/tp_ puppets.htm**

Seed garden: **www.freekidscrafts.com/seedling_ pot-e678.html**

Answer to question on page 22
The chair on the right is made from recycled cardboard.

Index